Everything in life is temporary. Alw
better days are ahead.

Always fall asleep with a dream. It will allow you to wake up with purpose.

Everything happens for a reason and someday it will all make perfect sense.

Know that you can move mountains if you really want something.

_____

_____

_____

_____

_____

_____

_____

_____

_____

_____

_____

_____

_____

_____

_____

_____

Today throw kindness around like confetti.

Never cease to be curious.

Stop living to please others and you'll feel empowered.

Don't imitate. You were born an original.

Never lose hope.

Recipe for today: Stress less, laugh more.

Make yourself time each day to find a quiet spot to breathe.

Today remember to enjoy little things.

Don't destroy your inner peace by letting other people destroy it with their acts.

Nobody can stop you if you know where you're going.

Remember to be thankful.

Don't let small failures deter you from your path.

You are braver than you believe.

_____

_____

_____

_____

_____

_____

_____

_____

_____

_____

_____

_____

_____

_____

_____

_____

_____

Remember to enjoy little things.

You only have today. Make it amazing!

Take pride in how far you've come.

Stay humble.

Never stop learning,

Never let your emotions overpower your intelligence.

Remember to be kind and work hard.

Never assume that quiet is weak.

Choose to do what is right, not what is easy.

_____

_____

_____

_____

_____

_____

_____

_____

_____

_____

_____

_____

_____

_____

_____

_____

_____

The enemy is fear. Be bold!

Remember that all frustrations are self-induced.

You attract in your life what you're ready for.

_____

_____

_____

_____

_____

_____

_____

_____

_____

_____

_____

_____

_____

_____

_____

_____

_____

Trust your intuition and never apologize for doing so.

Remember that you'll learn the greatest lessons from the worst mistakes.

Be the hustler, and go-getter.

Keep reminding yourself everything happens for a reason.

_____

_____

_____

_____

_____

_____

_____

_____

_____

_____

_____

_____

_____

_____

_____

_____

_____

_____

_____

_____

_____

Today wear your confidence. It is the most beautiful
thing you have.

_____

_____

_____

_____

_____

_____

_____

_____

_____

_____

_____

_____

_____

_____

_____

_____

_____

_____

Write your dreams with a date, then they will become goals.

Stay focused and surround yourself with good people.

Start the day with a new mindset and you'll get new results.

Say yes to new adventures.

Stop doubting yourself.

Don't look in any direction but ahead.

Take risks and remember that even if you lose, you'll be wiser.

Use your intuition as your superpower.

Remember this: You can start over, each day!

Sometimes things fall into place when they are falling apart.

Nourish your inner artist each and every day.

Don't stop what you're doing until you're proud.

Lifting others will rise you!

Look fear in the eye, and do what you want.

Remember to rest when you're tired. Don't quit!

Choose to be grateful no matter what.

Live with more intent.

Fill your day with laughter.

Do everything with great love. Even the smallest ones. It will change everything.

Don't focus on the mistakes. Focus on the lessons you learned.

You'll be unstoppable when you believe in yourself.

Seize the day, seize the opportunity!

Stop waiting, make the most of the moment you're in.

You have the power to make your future better!

Stop underestimating yourself

Always make time for yourself and don't stress over things you can't control.

Use today as another chance to get better.

You are amazing as you are!

Your life will become limitless once you become fearless.

Look at ordinary things and find joy in them.

Be patient. Everything will come to you in the right moment.

Be gentle with yourself.

Never forget to get up and fight again.

Choose happiness. Because you're in charge of how you feel!

Don't give up on things that set your soul on fire.

Remember this: Some things take time...

Don't change your goal when the plan doesn't work. Just change the plan.

Don't be concerned about your speed. Forward is forward!

Learn to embrace the storms of your life.

Give yourself a pep talk. Say "You got this and I love you!"

_____

_____

_____

_____

_____

_____

_____

_____

_____

_____

_____

_____

_____

_____

_____

_____

_____

Be a goal digger.

Don't overthink it!

You are halfway there. Keep on!

Try! Every accomplishment starts with the decision to try.

Be proud of yourself in each step you take towards your goal.

Be your authentic self.

Be courageous to step out of your comfort zone.

You were born to stand out!

Believe in your ability to succeed.

Stay positive and make it happen.

Today do more of what makes you happy.

Your mindset is everything. Exhale the past!

Remember this: You can't have a rainbow without a little rain in your life.

Focus on where you want to go.

Clear your mind of self doubt and embrace the challenge.

Follow your passion. Let it take you to the places!

You're not lost just because your path is different.

You'll always see the best view after the hardest climb.

Look at things in your life closer to find the blessings in disguise.

Start loving yourself for everything you already are.

Remember this: Hard is not impossible!

Never stop believing something wonderful is about to happen.

If you have many mistakes, then you have proofs that you have been trying!

Dream it, believe it and you'll achieve it!

Fill in these pages with what you've learned so far. Let your wisdom speak.

_____

_____

_____

_____

_____

_____

_____

_____

_____

_____

_____

_____

_____

_____

_____

_____

_____

_____

_____

Fill in these pages with what you've learned so far. Let your wisdom speak.

_____

_____

_____

_____

_____

_____

_____

_____

_____

_____

_____

_____

_____

_____

_____

_____

_____

_____

Fill in these pages with what you've learned so far. Let your wisdom speak.

_____

_____

_____

_____

_____

_____

_____

_____

_____

_____

_____

_____

_____

_____

_____

_____

_____

_____

_____

Fill in these pages with what you've learned so far. Let your wisdom speak.

_____

_____

_____

_____

_____

_____

_____

_____

_____

_____

_____

_____

_____

_____

_____

_____

_____

_____

_____

Fill in these pages with what you've learned so far. Let your wisdom speak.

_____

_____

_____

_____

_____

_____

_____

_____

_____

_____

_____

_____

_____

_____

_____

_____

_____

_____

Fill in these pages with what you've learned so far. Let your wisdom speak.

_____

_____

_____

_____

_____

_____

_____

_____

_____

_____

_____

_____

_____

_____

_____

_____

_____

_____

Fill in these pages with what you've learned so far. Let your wisdom speak.

Fill in these pages with what you've learned so far. Let your wisdom speak.

_____

_____

_____

_____

_____

_____

_____

_____

_____

_____

_____

_____

_____

_____

_____

_____

_____

_____

_____

_____

Fill in these pages with what you've learned so far. Let your wisdom speak.

Fill in these pages with what you've learned so far. Let your wisdom speak.

_____

_____

_____

_____

_____

_____

_____

_____

_____

_____

_____

_____

_____

_____

_____

_____

_____

_____

_____

Fill in these pages with what you've learned so far. Let your wisdom speak.

Fill in these pages with what you've learned so far. Let your wisdom speak.

Fill in these pages with what you've learned so far. Let your wisdom speak.

_____

_____

_____

_____

_____

_____

_____

_____

_____

_____

_____

_____

_____

_____

_____

_____

_____

_____

_____

_____

Fill in these pages with what you've learned so far. Let your wisdom speak.

_____

_____

_____

_____

_____

_____

_____

_____

_____

_____

_____

_____

_____

_____

_____

_____

_____

_____

Fill in these pages with what you've learned so far. Let your wisdom speak.

_____

_____

_____

_____

_____

_____

_____

_____

_____

_____

_____

_____

_____

_____

_____

_____

_____

_____

_____

Fill in these pages with what you've learned so far. Let your wisdom speak.

Fill in these pages with what you've learned so far. Let your wisdom speak.

Fill in these pages with what you've learned so far. Let your wisdom speak.

_____

_____

_____

_____

_____

_____

_____

_____

_____

_____

_____

_____

_____

_____

_____

_____

_____

_____

_____

Fill in these pages with what you've learned so far. Let your wisdom speak.

Fill in these pages with what you've learned so far. Let your wisdom speak.

31787034R00069

Made in the USA
San Bernardino, CA
08 April 2019